Food +
Farming

Meredith Hooper
is an acclaimed author of children's books –
novels, picture books and non-fiction – that appeal to all ages.
She specialises in science, technology
and history. Her previous books for Frances Lincoln are
The Pebble in my Pocket, The Drop in my Drink,
Tom Crean's Rabbit, Dogs' Night, Antarctic Journal, Ice Trap!, Ponko and the South Pole,
The Island that Moved and *Celebrity Cat*. The recipe for honey biscuits has been handed
down through the generations in Meredith's own family.

Alison Bartlett's
previous books for children include
Bob the Dog, Cat among the Cabbages and *Oliver's Vegetables,*
which was Highly Commended by the V&A Illustration Awards.
This is her first title for Frances Lincoln.
Alison lives with her family in Bath.

To my mother and her honey biscuits – M.H.
For Richard and Rachel, with much love – A.B.

Honey Biscuits copyright © Frances Lincoln Limited 2004
Text copyright © Meredith Hooper 1997
Illustrations copyright © Alison Bartlett 1997

First published in Great Britain in 1997 by Kingfisher

This edition published in Great Britain in 2004 by
Frances Lincoln Children's Books, 4 Torriano Mews,
Torriano Avenue, London NW5 2RZ
www.franceslincoln.com

British Library Cataloguing in Publication Data available on request

ISBN 978-1-84507-045-8

Printed in Singapore

3 5 7 9 8 6 4

honey biscuits

Meredith Hooper

Illustrated by Alison Bartlett

F

FRANCES LINCOLN
CHILDREN'S BOOKS

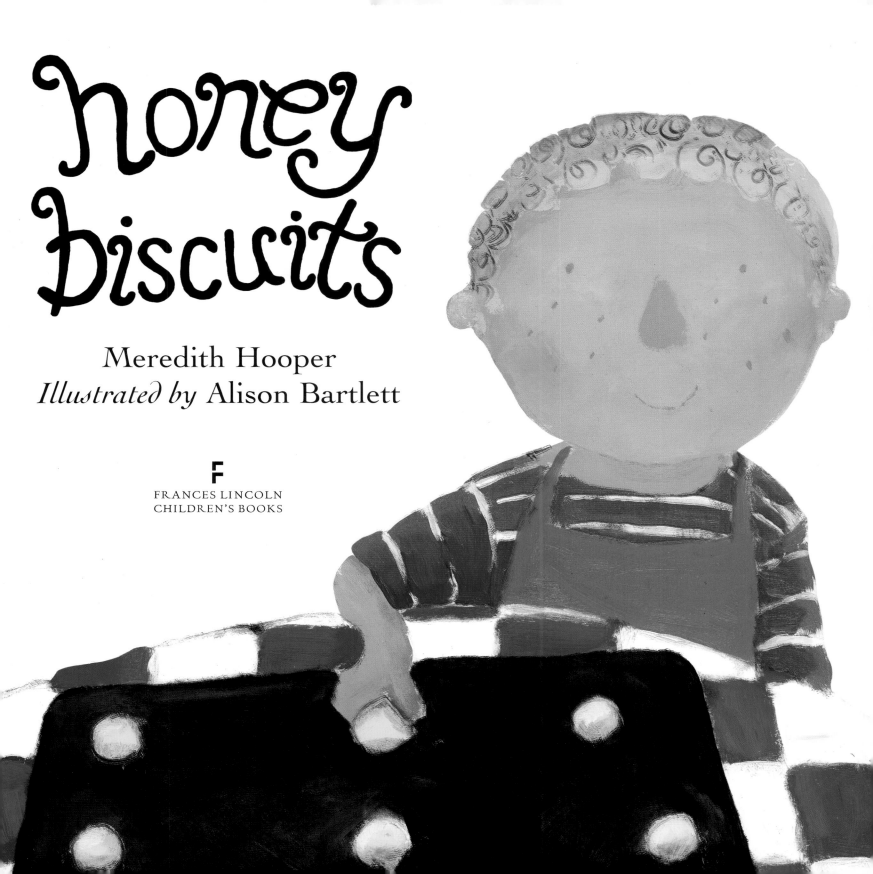

Ben was cooking with his gran.
"What shall we make?" asked Ben.
"Honey biscuits," said Gran.

"What do we need?" asked Ben.
"We need . . ." said Gran,

"A cow in a field eating fresh green grass,

munch,

dribble,

munch, all day long."

"A cow?" said Ben. "And grass! For honey biscuits?"
"Oh yes!" said Gran. "The cow turns the grass into creamy milk."

"Shake the milk round and round and it turns into smooth yellow butter."

"And 120 grams of smooth yellow butter is exactly what we need."

And now we need . . .

"Sugar cane
growing thick and tall in the warm moist earth,

till it's way, way above your head,

and as
thick as
your
wrist."

"Then it's crushed and cleaned
and boiled until it turns into
shiny little grains of
white sugar."

"And 120 grams of shiny
white sugar," said Gran,
"is exactly what we need."

"Mix the butter and
sugar together in a bowl
until they are smooth,"
said Gran.
"The butter mustn't
be too hard.
It should be
nice and soft."

"What do we need now?"
asked Ben.

"A thousand buzzing bees," said Gran, "working all day, sucking sweet nectar from flowers, then flying back

to their hives and packing the nectar into little waxy cells where it changes into runny honey."

"And one large tablespoonful of runny honey," said Gran, "is exactly what we need."

"And now we need . . .

"A clucky hen,
scratching around all day,

pecking up seeds and worms and tiny grubs.

"She eats two handfuls of wheat,
some scraps from the kitchen
and a spoonful of special food."

"Then, every morning, she lays an egg."

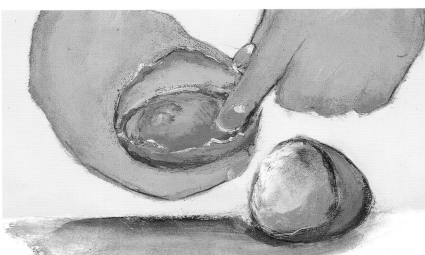

"But we don't need all of the egg," said Gran. "We just need the yellow part, the yolk."

"Put the runny honey into the bowl with the butter and sugar and beat it in," said Gran. "Now, here comes the tricky bit. Separating the yellow yolk from the clear part, the white, isn't easy."

"You just have to learn
by doing it."

"Put the egg yolk
into the mixture,"
said Gran,
"and beat it in."

"Now what do we need?"
asked Ben.

"Some dried bark," said Gran, "from a faraway tree."

"Bark?" said Ben,
"I don't want to eat bark!"
"It's called cinnamon, and
cinnamon's a spice," said Gran.
"Honey and spice make
something nice. Wait and see!"

"The bark is ground up into brown powder."

"And that's exactly what we need," said Gran, "a level teaspoonful of powdery brown cinnamon."

"And now we need . . .

"A field of golden wheat,

with ears full of seeds ripening in the sun."

"Grind up the seeds
and you get
soft white flour."

"And 180 grams of
soft white flour,"
said Gran,
" is exactly what we need."

"Put the cinnamon into the mixture," said Gran.
"Then add the flour bit by bit, but don't beat it for too long."

"Now we've made a stiff dough.
Here comes the good part. Ready?"

"Take a small piece of dough, roll it quickly in your hands,

and make a little ball."

"Roll the ball in some shiny white sugar and cinnamon."

"Then put it on the baking tray."

"You've got to give each little ball a bit of space," said Gran.
"Why?" asked Ben.
"Wait and see," said Gran.

"Remember, the oven mustn't be too hot, or too cool. It has to be just right to cook honey biscuits." Gran pulled on the oven gloves and put the tray of little balls in the oven.

Soon, a wonderful cooking smell filled the kitchen.

"Let's have a peep," said Gran. "We need to see how our honey biscuits are getting on." The little balls had disappeared. They had turned into round, flat golden-brown biscuits. Gran put on her oven gloves and took the hot tray out of the oven.

"Let the honey biscuits cool, just for a minute or two," said Gran.

"My honey biscuits,"
said Ben,
"have needed
a cow,
a thousand bees,
and a hen . . .

a field of sugar cane,
a field of wheat,
and part of a tree."

"And we've needed
the help of
fresh green grass and
bright coloured flowers,"
said Gran.

"And we've needed
the good earth,
the warm sun,
and the rain."

 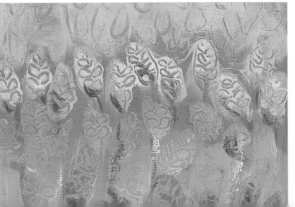 

But Ben couldn't
say anything.
His mouth
was too full of
lovely warm

honey
biscuit.

Honey Biscuits

To make honey biscuits, you need:
120 grams or ½ cup butter
120 grams or ⅔ cup sugar
1 large tablespoon honey (2 if using cup measurements)
1 egg yolk
1 level teaspoon cinnamon
180 grams or 1¾ cups self-raising flour

- Beat the butter and sugar together in a bowl until they are creamy. (You can use an electric mixer.)
- Next, beat in the honey, then the egg yolk.
- Add the cinnamon and flour and mix into a soft dough. If the dough is sticky, add a little more flour.
- Shape about a teaspoon of dough into a ball, roll it in a little sugar and cinnamon, and put it on a greased baking tray or cookie sheet. The mixture should make about 30 biscuits.
- Put the biscuits into an oven heated to 175 C, 350 F or gas mark 4, for 12 to 15 minutes.

The biscuits are ready when they are golden-brown. Take the biscuits out of the oven, let them settle for a few minutes, then put them on to a rack or a plate to cool.

MORE TITLES BY MEREDITH HOOPER
FROM FRANCES LINCOLN CHILDREN'S BOOKS

Tom Crean's Rabbit
A True Story from Scott's Last Voyage
Illustrated by Bert Kitchen

It's very cold in Antarctica, and Tom the sailor is looking for a quiet,
cosy place on the ship for his pet rabbit. Based on diaries
of men who sailed on board the *Terra Nova*.

*"A delightful information story that can be read for sheer
enjoyment and inspiration"* – Books for Keeps

ISBN 978-1-84507-393-0

Dogs' Night
With paintings from the National Gallery
Illustrated by Alan Curless

On one special night every year, the dogs in the paintings
in the National Gallery come to life. This is the fun-filled story
of the mayhem that ensues when, one year, they climb back
into the wrong pictures.

*"A witty book that is like a wonderful game and one that won't just
encourage a love of reading, but a love of looking too"* – The Guardian

ISBN 978-1-84507-688-7

Frances Lincoln titles are available from all good bookshops.
You can also buy books and find out more about your favourite titles,
authors and illustrators on our website: www.franceslincoln.com